Diabetic Side Dish

Cookbook

40 Easy and Healthy Diabetic Recipes for the Newly Diagnosed to Manage Prediabetes and Type 2 Diabetes

Melissa Mitchell

Table of Contents

Introduction

Diabetes Mellitus ("diabetes" for short) is a severe disease that occurs when your body has difficulty properly regulating the amount of dissolved sugar (glucose) in your bloodstream. It is unrelated to a similarly named disorder, "Diabetes Insipidus", which involves kidney-related fluid retention problems.

To understand diabetes, it is necessary first to understand the role glucose plays in the body and what can happen when glucose regulation fails. Blood sugar levels become dangerously low or high.

The tissues and cells that make up the human body are living things and require food to stay alive. The food cells eat a type of sugar called glucose. Fixed in place as they are, the body's cells are entirely dependent on the bloodstream in which they are bathed to bring glucose to them. Without access to adequate glucose, the body's cells have nothing to fuel themselves with and soon die.

Human beings eat food, not glucose. Human foods get converted into glucose as a part of the normal digestion process. Once converted, glucose enters the bloodstream, causing dissolved glucose inside the blood to rise. The bloodstream then carries the dissolved glucose to the various tissues and cells of the body.

Though glucose may be available in the blood, nearby cells cannot access that glucose without the aid of a chemical hormone called insulin. Insulin acts as a key to open the cells, allowing them to receive and utilize available glucose. Cells absorb glucose from the blood in the presence of insulin, and blood sugar levels drop as sugar leaves the blood and enters the cells. Insulin can be thought of as a bridge for glucose between the bloodstream and cells.

The body is designed to regulate and buffer the amount of glucose dissolved in the blood to maintain a steady supply to meet cell needs. The pancreas, one of your body's many organs, produces, stores, and releases insulin into the bloodstream to bring glucose levels back down.

The concentration of glucose available in the bloodstream at any given moment is dependent on the amount and type of foods that people eat. Refined carbohydrates, candy, and sweets are easy to break down into glucose. Correspondingly, blood glucose levels rise rapidly after such foods have been eaten. In contrast, blood sugars rise gradually and slowly after eating more complex, unrefined carbohydrates (oatmeal, apples, baked potatoes, etc.), which require more digestive steps to take place before glucose can be yielded. Faced with rapidly rising blood glucose concentrations, the body must react quickly by releasing large amounts of insulin at once or risk a dangerous condition called Hyperglycemia (high blood sugar) which will be described below.

The influx of insulin enables cells to utilize glucose, and glucose concentrations drop. While glucose levels can rise and fall rapidly, insulin levels change much more slowly. When a large amount of simple sugar is eaten, the bloodstream quickly becomes flooded with glucose. The pancreas releases insulin in response to the increased sugar. The glucose rapidly enters the cells, but the high insulin levels remain in the bloodstream for some time.

This can result in an overabundance of insulin in the blood, which can trigger feelings of hunger and even hypoglycemia (low blood sugar), another serious condition. When blood glucose concentrations rise more gradually, there is less need for dramatic compensation. Insulin can be released in a more controlled and safer manner, requiring the body to experience less strain. This more gradual process will leave you feeling "full" or content for a more extended period.

For these reasons, it is best for overall health to limit the amount and frequency of sweets and refined sugars in your diet. Instead, eat more complex sugars such as raw fruit, whole wheat bread and pasta, and beans. The difference between simple and complex sugars (carbohydrates) is exemplified by the difference between white (simple) and whole wheat (more difficult) bread.

Insulin is the critical key to the cell's ability to use glucose. Problems with insulin production or how insulin is recognized by the cells can easily cause the body's carefully balanced glucose metabolism system to get out of control. When either of these problems occurs, diabetes develops, blood sugar levels surge and crash, and the body risks becoming damaged.

Diabetes: Definition, Causes, And Symptoms

What Is Diabetes?

Diabetes is a disease that affects your body's ability to produce or use insulin. Insulin is a hormone. When your body turns the food you eat into energy (also called sugar or glucose), insulin is released to help transport this energy to the cells. Insulin acts as a "key." Its chemical message tells the cell to open and receive glucose. If you produce little or no insulin or are insulin resistant, too much sugar remains in your blood. Blood glucose levels are higher than average for individuals with diabetes. There are two main types of diabetes: Type 1 and Type 2.

Diabetes is a disease that occurs when your blood glucose, also called blood sugar, is too high. Blood glucose is your primary source of energy and comes from the food you eat. Insulin, a hormone made by the pancreas, helps glucose from food get into your cells to be used for energy. Sometimes your body doesn't make enough or any insulin or doesn't use insulin well. Glucose then stays in your blood and doesn't reach your cells.

What Is Type 1 Diabetes?

When you are affected with Type 1 diabetes, your pancreas does not produce insulin. Type 1 diabetes, once called juvenile diabetes, is often diagnosed in children or teens. However, it can also occur in adults. This type accounts for 5-10 percent of people with diabetes.

What Is Type 2 Diabetes?

Type 2 diabetes occurs when the body does not produce enough insulin or when the cells cannot use insulin properly, which is called insulin resistance. Type 2 diabetes is commonly called "adult-onset diabetes" since it is diagnosed later in life, generally after 45. It accounts for 90-95 percent of people with diabetes. In recent years, Type 2 diabetes has been diagnosed in younger people, including children, more frequently than in the past.

Gestational Diabetes

Gestational diabetes develops in some women when they are pregnant. Most of the time, this type of diabetes goes away after the baby is born. However, if you've had gestational diabetes, you have a greater chance of developing type 2 diabetes later in life. Sometimes diabetes diagnosed during pregnancy is type 2 diabetes.

Who Gets Diabetes? What Are The Risk Factors?

Factors that increase your risk differ depending on the type of diabetes you ultimately develop.

Risk Factors For Type 1 Diabetes Include:

- We are having a family history (parent or sibling) of type 1 diabetes.
- Injury to the pancreas (such as by infection, tumor, surgery, or accident).
- Presence of autoantibodies (antibodies that mistakenly attack your own body's tissues or organs).
- Physical stress (such as surgery or illness).
- Exposure to illnesses caused by viruses.

Risk Factors For Prediabetes And Type 2 Diabetes Include:

- Family history (parent or sibling) of prediabetes or type 2 diabetes.
- I am African-American, Hispanic, Native American, Asian-American race, or Pacific Islander.
- It is overweight.
- I had high blood pressure.
- I am having low HDL cholesterol (the "good" cholesterol) and a high triglyceride level.
- She was physically inactive.
- They were being aged 45 or older.

- I am having gestational diabetes or giving birth to a baby weighing more than 9 pounds.
- I have polycystic ovary syndrome.
- I was having a history of heart disease or stroke.
- She is a smoker.

Risk Factors For Gestational Diabetes Include:

- Family history (parent or sibling) of prediabetes or type 2 diabetes.
- Being African-American, Hispanic, Native American, or Asian-American.
- You are overweight before your pregnancy.
- They are over 25 years of age.

Symptoms And Causes

What Causes Diabetes?

The cause of diabetes, regardless of the type, is having too much glucose circulating in your bloodstream. However, the reason why your blood glucose levels are high differs depending on the type of diabetes.

1. Causes Of Type 1 Diabetes: This is an immune system disease. Your body attacks and destroys insulin-producing cells in your pancreas. Without insulin to allow glucose to enter your cells, glucose builds up in your bloodstream. Genes may also play a role in some patients. Also, a virus may trigger an immune system attack.

2. Cause Of Type 2 Diabetes And Prediabetes: Your body's cells don't allow insulin to work as it should to let glucose into its cells. Your body's cells have become resistant to insulin. Your pancreas can't keep up and make enough insulin to overcome this resistance. Glucose levels rise in your bloodstream.

3. Gestational Diabetes: Hormones produced by the placenta during pregnancy make your body's cells more resistant to insulin. Your pancreas can't make enough insulin to overcome this resistance. Too much glucose remains in your bloodstream.

What Causes Diabetes?

Genetics, lifestyle, and environment can be causes of diabetes. Eating an unhealthy diet, being overweight or obese, and not exercising enough may play a role in developing diabetes, particularly Type 2 diabetes. An autoimmune response causes type 1 diabetes. The body's immune system attacks and destroys the insulin-producing beta cells in the pancreas.

How Does Diabetes Affect My Body?

Over time, high blood sugar levels (also called hyperglycemia) can lead to kidney disease, heart disease, and blindness. The excess sugar in the bloodstream can damage the tiny blood vessels in your eyes and kidneys and can harden or narrow your arteries.

What Are The Symptoms Of Diabetes?

- Extreme thirst
- Frequent urination
- Blurry vision
- Extreme hunger
- Increased tiredness
- Unusual weight loss

What Health Problems Can People With Diabetes Develop?

Over time, high blood glucose leads to problems such as:

- Heart disease
- Stroke
- Kidney disease
- Eye problems
- Dental disease
- Nerve damage
- Foot problems

You can take steps to lower your chances of developing these diabetes-related health problems.

How Can I Find Out If I Have Diabetes?

Sometimes a routine exam by an eye doctor or foot doctor will reveal diabetes. Diabetes affects the circulation to your feet and the tiny blood vessels in your eyes. If your eye doctor or your foot doctor suspects you have diabetes, they will recommend seeing your regular physician for a blood sugar level test. The most common test is a fasting blood glucose test. After not eating for at least eight hours, your doctor will usually take a blood sample overnight. The standard, non-diabetic range for fasting blood glucose is 70 to 110 mg/dl. If your level is 126 mg/dl or greater, you may have diabetes.

How Is Diabetes Managed?

Diabetes affects your whole body. To best manage diabetes, you'll need to take steps to keep your risk factors under control and within the normal range, including:

- Keep your blood glucose levels as near to normal as possible by following a diet plan, taking prescribed medication, and increasing your activity level.
- Maintain your blood cholesterol (HDL and LDL levels) and triglyceride levels near the normal ranges as possible.
- Control your blood pressure. Your blood pressure should not be over 140/90 mmHg.

You hold the keys to managing your diabetes by:

We are planning what you eat and following a healthy meal plan. Follow a Mediterranean diet (vegetables, whole grains, beans, fruits, healthy fats, low sugar) or Dash diet. These diets are high in nutrition and fiber and low in fats and calories. See a registered dietitian for help understanding nutrition and meal planning.

- I am exercising regularly. Try to exercise for at least 30 minutes most days of the week. Walk, swim or find some activity you enjoy.
- You are losing weight if you are overweight. Work with your healthcare team to develop a weight-loss plan.
- Taking medication and insulin, if prescribed, and closely following recommendations on how and when to take it.
- We are monitoring your blood glucose and blood pressure levels at home.
- You are keeping your appointments with your healthcare providers and having laboratory tests completed as ordered by your doctor.
- I am quitting smoking (if you smoke).
- You have a lot of control – on a day-to-day basis – in managing your diabetes!

How Do I Check My Blood Glucose Level? Why Is This Important?

Checking your blood glucose level is essential because the results help guide decisions about what to eat, your physical activity, and any needed medication and insulin adjustments or additions.

The most common way to check your blood glucose level is with a blood glucose meter. With this test, you prick the side of your finger, apply the drop of blood to a test strip, insert the strip into the meter, and the meter will show your glucose level at that moment in time. Your healthcare provider will tell you how often you'll need to check your glucose level.

What Is Continuous Glucose Monitoring?

Advancements in technology have given us another way to monitor glucose levels. Continuous glucose monitoring uses a tiny sensor inserted under your skin. You don't need to prick your finger. Instead, the sensor measures your glucose and can display results anytime during the day or night. Ask your healthcare provider about continuous glucose monitors to see if this is an option for you.

What Should My Blood Glucose Level Be?

Ask your healthcare team what your blood glucose level should be. They may have a specific target range for you. In general, though, most people try to keep their blood glucose levels at these targets:

- **Before A Meal:** between 80 and 130 mg/dL.
- **About Two Hours After The Start Of A Meal**: Less than 180 mg/dL.

What Happens If My Blood Glucose Level Is Low?

Having a lower blood glucose level than the normal range (usually below 70 mg/dL) is called hypoglycemia. This is a sign that your body gives out that you need sugar. Symptoms you might experience if you have hypoglycemia include:

- Weakness or shaking
- Moist skin, sweating
- Fast heartbeat
- Dizziness
- Sudden hunger
- Confusion
- Pale skin
- Numbness in mouth or tongue
- Irritability, nervousness
- Unsteadiness
- Nightmares, bad dreams, restless sleep
- Blurred vision
- Headaches, seizures
- You might pass out if your hypoglycemia is not managed

What Happens If My Blood Glucose Level Is High?

If you have too much glucose in your blood, you have a condition called Hyperglycemia. Hyperglycemia is defined as:

- A blood glucose level greater than 125 mg/dL while in the fasting state (nothing to eat or drink for at least eight hours).

  or

- A blood glucose level greater than 180 mg/dL one to two hours after eating.

How Is Diabetes Treated?

Treatments for diabetes depend on your type of diabetes, how well controlled your blood glucose level is, and your other existing health conditions.

1. Type 1 Diabetes: If you have this type, you must take insulin every day. Your pancreas no longer makes insulin.

2. Type 2 Diabetes: If you have this type, your treatments can include medications (both for diabetes and for conditions that are risk factors for diabetes), insulin, and lifestyle changes such as losing weight, making healthy food choices, and being more physically active.

3. Prediabetes: If you have prediabetes, the goal is to keep you from progressing to diabetes. Treatments are focused on treatable risk factors, such as losing weight by eating a healthy diet (like the Mediterranean diet) and exercising (at least five days a week for 30 minutes).

4. Gestational Diabetes: If you have this type and your glucose level is not too high, your initial treatment might modify your diet and get regular exercise. If the target goal is still not met or your glucose level is very high, your healthcare team may start medication or insulin.

Oral Medications And Insulin Work In One Of These Ways To Treat Your Diabetes:

- Stimulates your pancreas to make and release more insulin.
- Slows down the release of glucose from your liver (extra glucose is stored in your liver).
- Blocks the breakdown of carbohydrates in your stomach or intestines so that your tissues are more sensitive to (better react to) insulin.
- Helps rid your body of glucose through increased urination.

What Types Of Diabetes Require Insulin?

People with type 1 diabetes need insulin to live. If you have type 1 diabetes, your body has attacked your pancreas, destroying the cells that make insulin. If you have type 2 diabetes, your pancreas makes insulin, but it doesn't work as it should. In some people with type 2 diabetes, insulin may be needed to help glucose move from your bloodstream to your body's cells, where it's necessary for energy. You may or may not need insulin if you have gestational diabetes. Suppose you are pregnant or have type 2 diabetes. In that case, your healthcare provider will check your blood glucose level, assess other risk factors and determine a treatment approach that may include a combination of lifestyle changes, oral medications, and insulin. Each person is unique, and so is your treatment plan.

How Insulin Works In The Body

Insulin is a hormone produced by the pancreas to help metabolize and use food for energy throughout the body. This is a critical biological function, so a problem with insulin can have a widespread effect on any or all of the body's tissues, organs, and systems. Insulin is so essential to overall health and even survival that when there are problems with insulin production or utilization, as with diabetes, supplemental insulin often is needed throughout the day. In fact, in type 1 diabetes, an autoimmune disease in which the body produces no insulin, supplemental insulin is vital. Extra insulin isn't always necessary for treating type 2 diabetes, the form of diabetes in which insulin production is lower than usual, and the body cannot use it efficiently. This inefficient use of insulin is called insulin resistance.

If you have either type of diabetes, learning how the naturally produced hormone works in the body can help you understand why taking daily insulin shots or wearing an insulin pump or patch may be an essential aspect of your treatment plan.

How Insulin Is Produced

Insulin is produced by the pancreas, a glandlike organ nestled in the curve of the duodenum (the first part of the small intestine), just behind the stomach. The pancreas functions both as an exocrine gland and an endocrine gland. The exocrine function of the pancreas is to help with digestion. It's in the role of an endocrine gland that the pancreas produces insulin and another hormone called glucagon.

Insulin is produced by specialized beta cells in the pancreas, clustered into groups called islets of Langerhans. There are approximately one million islets in the healthy adult pancreas, taking up about 5% of the entire organ. (The pancreatic cells that produce glucagon are called alpha cells.)

How Insulin Works

Insulin is the energy storage hormone. After a meal, it helps the cells use carbs, fats, and protein as needed and to store what's left (mainly as fat) for the future. The body breaks these nutrients down into sugar molecules, amino acid molecules, and lipid molecules, respectively. The body also can store and reassemble these molecules into more complex forms.

Carbohydrate Metabolism

Blood sugar levels rise when most foods are consumed, but they grow more rapidly and dramatically with carbohydrates. The digestive system releases glucose from foods, and the glucose molecules are absorbed into the bloodstream. The rising glucose levels signal the pancreas to secrete insulin to clear glucose from the bloodstream. To do this, insulin binds with insulin receptors on the surface of cells, acting like a key that opens the cells to receive glucose. There are insulin receptors on almost all tissues in the body, including muscle cells and fat cells.

Insulin receptors have two main components, the exterior and interior portions. The exterior portion extends outside the cell and binds with insulin. When this happens, the internal part of the receptor sends out a signal inside the cell for glucose transporters to mobilize to the surface and receive the glucose. As blood sugar and insulin levels decrease, the receptors empty, and the glucose transporters go back into the cell. When the body is functioning normally, the glucose derived from ingested carbohydrates gets cleared rapidly through this process.

Excess blood sugar also results when cells aren't able to use insulin properly. Insulin resistance can be due to a problem with the shape of the insulin (preventing receptor binding), not having enough insulin receptors, signaling problems, or glucose transporters not working correctly.

Fat Metabolism

Insulin has a significant effect on fat metabolism. After a meal, insulin causes "extra" ingested fats and glucose to be stored as fat for future use.

Insulin Also Plays A Crucial Role In:

The Liver: Insulin stimulates the creation and storage of glycogen from glucose. High insulin levels cause the liver to get saturated with glycogen. When this happens, the liver resists further storage. Glucose is used instead to create fatty acids that are converted into lipoproteins and released into the bloodstream. These break down into free fatty acids and are used in other tissues. Some tissues use these to create triglycerides.

Fat Cells: Insulin stops the breakdown of fat and prevents the breakdown of triglycerides into fatty acids. When glucose enters these cells, who can use it to create a compound called glycerol, glycerol can be combined with the excess free fatty acids from the liver to make triglycerides. This can cause triglycerides to build up in the fat cells.

Protein Metabolism

Insulin helps the amino acids in protein to enter cells. Without adequate insulin production, this process is hindered, making it difficult to build muscle mass.

Insulin also makes cells more receptive to potassium, magnesium, and phosphate. Known collectively as electrolytes, these minerals help conduct electricity within the body. In doing so, they influence muscle function, blood pH, and the amount of water in the body. An electrolyte imbalance can be worsened by high blood sugar levels as this can cause excessive urination (polyuria) with water and electrolyte loss.

Summarization

While insulin is primarily regarded as the hormone that regulates blood sugar, it also plays a crucial role in the metabolism of the protein and fats in the food we eat and how they're utilized and stored. For people with type 1 diabetes, the absence of insulin cannot be helped, but it can be managed with supplemental insulin. For others, there are ways to help prevent problems with insulin that could lead to type 2 diabetes, including following a balanced, nutrient-rich diet, maintaining a healthy weight, exercising regularly, and taking other measures to live an overall healthy lifestyle.

Eating Better And Exercising For Diabetes Management

Diet & Exercise

Nutrition and physical activity are essential parts of a healthy lifestyle, whether you have diabetes or not. Along with other benefits, following a healthy meal plan and being active can help you keep your blood glucose level, also called blood sugar, in your target range. To manage your blood glucose, you need to balance what you eat and drink with physical activity and diabetes medicine if you take any.

Becoming more active and making changes in what you eat and drink can seem challenging at first. It is easier to start with small changes and get help from your family, friends, and healthcare team. Eating well and being physically active most days of the week can help you:

- Keep your blood glucose level, blood pressure, and cholesterol in your target ranges.
- Lose weight or stay at a healthy weight
- Prevent or delay diabetes problems
- Feel good and have more energy

What Foods Can I Eat If I Have Diabetes?

Eat smaller portions. Learn about serving sizes and how many servings you need in a meal. The key to eating with diabetes is to eat various healthy foods from all food groups, in the amounts your meal plan specifies.

The Food Groups Are:

Vegetables

- **Non-Starchy:** Includes broccoli, carrots, greens, peppers, and tomatoes
- **Starchy:** Includes potatoes, corn, and green peas
- **Fruits:** Includes oranges, melon, berries, apples, bananas, and grapes
- **Grains:** At least half of your grains for the day should be whole grains

Includes wheat, rice, oats, cornmeal, barley, and quinoa

Examples: bread, pasta, cereal, and tortillas

Protein

- Lean meat
- Chicken or turkey without the skin
- Fish
- Eggs
- Nuts and peanuts
- Dried beans and sure peas, such as chickpeas and split peas
- Meat substitutes, such as tofu

Dairy: Nonfat or low fat

- Milk or lactose-free milk if you have lactose intolerance
- Yogurt
- Cheese

Eat foods with heart-healthy fats, which mainly come from these foods:

- Oils that are liquid at room temperature, such as olive oil
- Nuts and seeds
- Heart-healthy fish such as salmon, tuna, and mackerel
- Avocado
- Use oils when cooking food instead of butter, cream, shortening, lard, or stick margarine

What Foods And Drinks Should I Limit If I Have Diabetes?

Foods And Drinks To Limit Include:

- Fried foods and other foods high in saturated fat and trans fat
- Foods high in salt also called sodium
- Sweets, such as baked goods, candy, and ice cream
- Beverages with added sugars, such as juice, regular soda, and regular sports or energy drinks
- Drink water instead of sweetened beverages. Consider using a sugar substitute in your coffee or tea.

If you drink alcohol, drink moderately, no more than one drink a day if you're a woman, or two drinks a day if you're a man. If you use insulin or diabetes medicines that increase the amount of insulin your body makes, alcohol can make your blood glucose level drop too low.[1]

How Much Can I Eat If I Have Diabetes?

Two common ways to help you plan how much to eat if you have diabetes are plate and carbohydrate counting. Check with your health care team about the process that's best for you.

1. Plate Method

The plate method shows the amount of each food group you should eat. This method works best for lunch and dinner.

2. Carbohydrate Counting Method

Carb counting involves keeping track of the number of carbs you eat and drink each day. Because carbs turn into glucose in your body, they affect your blood glucose level more than other foods do. Carb counting can help you manage your blood glucose level. If you take insulin, counting carbs can help you know how much insulin to take.

Most carbs come from starches, fruits, milk, and sweets. Try to limit carbs with added sugars or refined grains, such as white bread and white rice. Instead, eat carbs from fruit, vegetables, whole grains, beans, and low-fat or nonfat milk.

Why Should I Be Physically Active If I Have Diabetes?

Physical activity is an integral part of managing your blood glucose level and staying healthy. Physical activity:

- Lowers blood glucose levels
- Lowers blood pressure
- Improves blood flow
- Burns extra calories so you can keep your weight down if needed
- Improves your mood
- Can prevent falls and improve memory in older adults

- It may help you sleep better.

What Physical Activities Should I Do If I Have Diabetes?

- Ask your health care team what physical activities are safe for you. Many people choose to walk with friends or family members.
- If you have been inactive or are trying a new activity, start slowly, with 5 to 10 minutes a day. Then add more time each week.
- Walk around while you talk on the phone or during TV commercials.
- Do chores, such as work in the garden, rake leaves, clean the house, or wash the car.
- Park at the far end of the shopping center parking lot and walk to the store.
- Take the stairs instead of the elevator.
- Make your family outings active, such as a family bike ride or a walk in the park.

Medication

Insulin and other diabetes medications are designed to lower your blood sugar levels when diet and exercise alone aren't sufficient for managing diabetes. But the effectiveness of these medications depends on the timing and size of the dose. Medicines you take for conditions other than diabetes also can affect your blood sugar levels.

What To Do:

1. Store Insulin Properly: Insulin that's improperly stored or past its expiration date may not be adequate. Insulin is especially sensitive to extremes in temperature.

2. Report Problems To Your Doctor: If your diabetes medications cause your blood sugar level to drop too low or if it's consistently too high, the dosage or timing may need to be adjusted.

3. Be Cautious With New Medications: If you're considering an over-the-counter medication or your doctor prescribes a new drug to treat another condition such as high blood pressure or high cholesterol, ask your doctor or pharmacist if the medication may affect your blood sugar levels.

Sometimes an alternate medication may be recommended. Always check with your doctor before taking any new over-the-counter medicines to know how they may impact your blood sugar level.

Illness

When you're sick, your body produces stress-related hormones that help your body fight the illness, but they also can raise your blood sugar level. Changes in your appetite and regular activity also may complicate diabetes management.

What To Do:

1. Plan Ahead: Work with your health care team to create a sick-day plan. Include instructions on what medications to take, how often to measure your blood sugar and urine ketone levels, how to adjust your medication dosages, and when to call your doctor.

2. Continue To Take Your Diabetes Medication: However, if you're unable to eat because of nausea or vomiting, contact your doctor. In these situations, you may need to adjust your insulin dose or temporarily reduce or withhold short-acting insulin or diabetes medication because of a risk of hypoglycemia. However, do not stop your long-acting insulin.

3. Stick To Your Diabetes Meal Plan: If you can, eating, as usual, will help you control your blood sugar levels. Keep a supply of foods that are easy on your stomachs, such as gelatin, crackers, soups, and applesauce. Drink lots of water or other fluids that don't add calories, such as tea, to make sure you stay hydrated. If you're taking insulin, you may need to sip sugar-sweetened beverages, such as juice or a sports drink to keep your blood sugar level from dropping too low.

RECIPES

1. Baked Plantain For Diabetics

Preparation Time: 5 Minutes

Baking Time: 45 Minutes

Ingredients

- Two large, ripe plantains (skin blackened)

Directions

1. Preheat oven to 350°F.

2. Wash and dry plantains. Trim off both ends of each plantain.

3. Make a slit in the peel of the plantain lengthwise.

4. Place on a baking sheet and bake for approximately 45 minutes (turning over halfway through the baking) until plantain flesh is tender.

5. Slice each plantain into three equal-sized pieces and serve in the skin.

Nutrition Information

- Carbohydrates: 19g, Protein: 1g, Sodium: 2mg, Fiber: 1g

2. Microwave Lima Bean Casserole

Preparation Time: 45 Minutes (Includes Cooking Time)

Ingredients

- 2 cups fresh or frozen lima beans
- Four slices of uncooked turkey bacon (optional)
- Vegetable cooking spray
- 1/2 cup dry bread crumbs
- Two tablespoons margarine, melted
- 2 cups chopped fresh tomatoes
- 1/4 teaspoon ground black pepper

- 1/4 teaspoon celery salt
- 1/4 cup chopped onion

Directions

1. Place lima beans in a microwave-safe dish with a small amount of water; microwave on high for 6 to 9 minutes, then let stand, covered, for 2 minutes.
2. Drain. Spread 3 or 4 paper towels on a plate, arrange bacon on the towels, and microwave on High for 3 minutes.
3. Test for crispness, and continue microwaving, if necessary, checking for doneness every 30 seconds. Spray a 6-cup casserole with cooking spray.
4. Mix bread crumbs with margarine in a large bowl. Add lima beans, tomatoes, pepper, salt, and onions. Pour mixture into casserole.
5. Microwave on High for 10 to 12 minutes, until the dish is bubbly.
6. Crumble bacon on top.

Nutrition Information

- Carbohydrates: 21g, Protein: 7g, Fat: 6g, Saturated Fat: 1g, Sodium: 360mg, Fiber: 5g

3. Polish Chilled Fish In Horseradish Sauce

Preparation Time: 50 Minutes

Ingredients

- Two carrots
- Two stalks celery
- One sprig parsley
- One onion, quartered
- Five peppercorns
- One bay leaf
- 6 cups water

- Eight four-ounce fish fillets (carp, sole, pike, or similar fish)
- Two tablespoons margarine
- Three tablespoons flour
- Two tablespoons prepared horseradish sauce
- One teaspoon sugar
- Dash salt
- 1/2 cup light sour cream
- Two eggs, hard-boiled, peeled and diced
- 1 cup shredded lettuce

Directions

1. Place carrots, celery, parsley, onion, peppercorns, bay leaf, and water in a large pot. Bring to a boil and simmer for 20 minutes.
2. Strain broth and add fish fillets to hot vegetable broth, cooking for 6–10 minutes until the fish flakes easily.
3. Remove fish from broth and arrange fillets on a serving platter: cover and chill.
4. Strain and chill 3/4 cup of the remaining fish broth, reserving it for the sauce.
5. In a saucepan, melt the margarine. Blend in flour until it forms a smooth paste.
6. Add the cooled fish broth gradually, stirring constantly.
7. Cook and stir until the sauce boils.

8. Remove from heat and stir in horseradish sauce, sugar, a dash of salt, sour cream, and chopped hard-boiled eggs.

9. Cool for 15 minutes. Pour the horseradish sauce over the chilled fish, garnish with shredded lettuce, and serve immediately.

Nutrition Information

- Carbohydrates: 5g, Protein: 24g, Fat: 6g, Saturated Fat: 2g, Sodium: 135mg,

4. Colorful Vegetable Casserole

Preparation Time: 15 Minutes

Baking Time: 1 Hour

Ingredients

- Vegetable cooking spray
- One package (16 ounces) of frozen Italian-mix vegetables
- One large green pepper, cut into strips
- 1 pound baby carrots, halved

- One medium zucchini, unpeeled, cut into 1/2-inch slices
- Four medium tomatoes, quartered
- 1 cup celery, sliced
- Two tablespoons butter or margarine
- 1 1/2 cups chopped onion
- Two large cloves of garlic, minced
- Two teaspoons instant reduced-sodium chicken broth granules
- Two tablespoons cooking wine
- 1/2 teaspoon salt
- 1/2 teaspoon pepper

Directions

1. Preheat oven to 325°F. Spray a 3-quart casserole or Dutch oven with cooking spray.
2. Spread frozen vegetables in an even layer in the soup. Follow with layers of green pepper strips, baby carrots, zucchini slices, tomato pieces, and celery.
3. Melt margarine in skillet. Add onion and garlic, sautéing until tender.
4. Stir in broth granules, wine, salt, and pepper. Pour skillet mixture over vegetables.
5. Cover casserole and bake for approximately 1 hour until vegetables are crisp-tender.

Nutrition Information

- Carbohydrates: 15g, Protein: 3g, Fat: 3g, Saturated Fat: <1g, Sodium: 227mg, Fiber: 4g

5. Spinach Almond Casserole

Preparation Time: 30 Minutes

Cooking Time: 30–35 Minutes.

Ingredients

- Two tablespoons sesame seeds
- 1/4 cup slivered almonds

- Two packages (10 ounces each) frozen chopped spinach
- 1/8 teaspoon black pepper
- One can (10 3/4 ounces) reduced-fat, low-sodium cream of mushroom soup concentrate
- 1/2 cup low-fat sour cream
- One can (8 ounces) sliced water chestnuts, drained
- Vegetable cooking spray

Directions

1. Toast sesame seeds and almonds in a skillet just until slightly browned.
2. Set aside. Cook spinach on the stove or in the microwave according to package directions, omitting salt.
3. Drain spinach thoroughly by placing it in a colander and pressing it with a large spoon.
4. In a large bowl, toss spinach with sesame seeds, almonds, pepper, soup, sour cream, and water chestnuts.
5. Spray one 1/2-quart casserole with cooking spray and spoon in spinach mixture.
6. Bake in a preheated 350°F oven for 30 to 35 minutes.

Nutrition Information

- Carbohydrates: 11g, Protein: 4g, Fat: 5g, Saturated Fat: 1g, Sodium: 207mg, Fiber: 3g

6. Greek Christmas Bread

Preparation Time: 45 Minutes

Rising Time: 1 1/2 Hours Total

Baking Time: 35–40 Minutes

Ingredients

- 1 1/2 tablespoons yeast
- 1/2 teaspoon sugar plus 1/3 cup sugar
- One tablespoon flour plus 3 1/2 cups flour (may require up to 1/2 cup additional flour to make a stiff dough)
- Dash salt
- 1/4 cup warm water
- Three eggs
- 3/4 cup nonfat milk, scalded and cooled
- 1/2 teaspoon vanilla flavoring
- 1/3 cup margarine, melted and cooled
- 1/2 cup slivered almonds
- 1/4 cup yellow raisins
- 1/2 teaspoon grated lemon peel

Directions

1. Combine yeast, 1/2 teaspoon sugar, one tablespoon flour, dash salt, and warm water in a bowl.

2. Let stand in a warm place for 10 minutes until the mixture is bubbly and foamy.

3. Add two eggs, 1/3 cup sugar, cooled milk, and vanilla, and stir well. Add melted margarine, almonds, raisins, and lemon peel.

4. Add 3 1/2 cups flour a little bit at a time, stirring until a stiff, elastic dough forms. (Add up to 1/2 cup more flour as needed.) Turn dough out onto the floured surface and knead for five minutes.

5. Place in an oiled bowl and cover with plastic wrap, then a damp towel.

6. Let dough rise in a warm place for about 30 minutes, then punch down and turn over.

7. Let rise again for 30 minutes until it is almost doubled in size. Shape into a round or oblong shape, place on a lightly oiled baking sheet, and let rise again for 30 minutes.

8. Beat the remaining egg and brush about half of the egg mixture on the top of the entire surface of the dough.

9. Discard leftover beaten egg and bake the bread at 350°F for approximately 35–40 minutes, until golden brown and done.

Nutrition Information

- Carbohydrates: 22g, Protein: 4g, Fat: 4g, Saturated Fat: 1g, Sodium: 53mg, Fiber: 1g

7. Fried Brown Rice For Diabetics

Preparation Time: 5 Minutes

Cooking Time: Approximately 10 Minutes.

Standing Time: 7 Minutes

Ingredients

- Cooking spray
- Two teaspoons reduced-calorie margarine
- 1/4 cup liquid egg substitute
- One chopped green onion
- 1 1/2 cups instant brown rice
- 1 1/2 cups 50% less sodium, fat-free chicken broth
- 1/2 cup frozen peas and carrots, unthawed (alternatively, who can use unthawed frozen mixed vegetables)

Directions

1. Coat a large, nonstick skillet with cooking spray; add margarine, and melt over medium heat.
2. Add egg substitute and stir-fry until egg is set (like scrambled egg).
3. Stir in onion, rice, broth, and peas, and carrots; stir to mix. Bring mixture to a boil over high heat, cover, reduce heat to medium-low, and simmer for 5 minutes.
4. Remove from the heat, stir, and body. Let stand 7 minutes, fluff with a fork, and serve.

Nutrition Information

- Carbohydrates: 16g, Protein: 4g, Fat: 2g, Saturated Fat: <1g, Sodium: 163mg, Fiber: 1g

8. Rich-Tasting Red Clam Sauce

Preparation Time: 10 Minutes

Cooking Time: 1 Hour And 5 Minutes.

Ingredients

- Two tablespoons olive oil
- 1/2 cup finely chopped onion
- Two large celery stalks, finely chopped
- Four cloves garlic, minced
- Two cans (14 1/2 ounces each) no-salt-added diced tomatoes
- One can (6 ounces) no-salt-added tomato paste
- Two cans (10 ounces each) whole clams, drained, with liquid reserved
- 1/8–1/4 teaspoon red pepper flakes
- Two teaspoons crushed dried oregano
- 1/4 teaspoon dried basil

Directions

1. Heat olive oil in a large saucepan over medium-high heat.
2. Add onion, celery, and garlic and cook, constantly stirring, until tender.

3. Stir in tomatoes, tomato paste, liquid from clams, red pepper flakes to taste, oregano, and basil.

4. Cover and simmer over low-medium heat for 50 minutes, or until tomatoes turn a deeper red and the sauce thickens; stir periodically to prevent sticking.

5. Stir in clams and simmer 10 minutes more.

6. Serve over rice or pasta. The sauce reheats well.

Nutrition Information

- Carbohydrates: 15g, Protein: 13g, Fat: 6g, Saturated Fat: 1g, Cholesterol: 440mg, Sodium: 3g, Fiber: 3g

9. Basmati Rice Pilaf

Preparation Time: About 1 Hour

Ingredients

- Two teaspoons olive oil
- Two cloves garlic, peeled and minced
- One large onion, peeled and finely chopped (1 cup)

- One teaspoon curry powder
- 4 cups water
- 2 cups basmati brown rice
- 1 cup frozen green peas, thawed
- 1 cup diced red pepper

Directions

1. Heat oil in a large saucepan or Dutch oven.
2. Add the garlic and onion, sautéing until tender.
3. Stir in the curry powder, stirring to combine with the vegetables.
4. Add water and bring ingredients to a boil.
5. Stir in the rice, reduce heat to low, cover the pan, and simmer rice for 40 to 45 minutes until the water is almost completely absorbed.
6. Add the peas and red pepper, and continue cooking the rice 5 minutes longer.

Nutrition Information

- Carbohydrates: 45g, Protein: 5g, Fat: 2g, Saturated Fat: <1g, Sodium: 17g, Fiber: 2g

10. Make-Ahead Mashed Potatoes

Preparation Time: 30 Minutes

Baking Time: 45 Minutes

Ingredients

- 3 pounds potatoes, peeled and quartered
- 1/2 cup fat-free sour cream
- 4 ounces fat-free cream cheese
- One tablespoon butter-flavor spray
- 1/2 teaspoon salt (optional)
- 1/8 teaspoon pepper
- Skim milk

Directions

1. Boil potatoes in water for about 20 minutes or until done. Drain water off and whip with a mixer until smooth.
2. Add sour cream, cream cheese, butter-flavor spray, salt, and pepper, mixing well after each addition. If the potatoes are too thick, add 1/4 to 1/2 cup skim milk for desired consistency.

3. Spray a 2-quart casserole pan with butter-flavor cooking spray and spread potatoes evenly in the pan. Cover and refrigerate. Who can make this recipe two to three days in advance?

4. When ready to use, bake at 350°F for 45 minutes or until hot.

Nutrition Information

- Carbohydrates: 24g, Protein: 5g, Sodium: 85mg

11. Savory Bread Dressing

Preparation Time: 20 Minutes

Baking Time: 30 Minutes

Ingredients

- Two tablespoons margarine
- 1/4 cup chopped onions

- 1/2 cup finely diced celery
- 8 cups herb-seasoned croutons for stuffing
- 1/4 teaspoon salt (optional)
- 1/4 teaspoon ground pepper
- 2 cups turkey or chicken broth
- One egg
- Cooking spray

Directions

1. Melt margarine in a large skillet. Add onion and celery; cook until tender.
2. Add croutons, salt, and pepper.
3. Moisten with broth. Beat egg with a fork and stir into dressing mixture.
4. Spray a 2-quart casserole with cooking spray and put the dressing in it.
5. Bake, covered, at 350°F for 30 minutes.

Nutrition Information

- Carbohydrates: 14g, Protein: 3g, Fat: 2g, Saturated Fat: 1g, Sodium: 276mg, Fiber: <1g

12. Turkey Gravy For Diabetics

Preparation Time: 20 Minutes

Ingredients

- Five tablespoons cornstarch
- Five tablespoons water
- 3 cups turkey or chicken broth, defatted
- Salt and pepper as desired

Directions

1. Mix cornstarch and water in a bowl until blended.
2. Place turkey broth in a 1-quart saucepan and bring to a boil over medium heat.
3. Slowly add the cornstarch mixture to the turkey broth, stirring until the gravy is thickened.
4. Season to taste with salt and pepper.

Nutrition Information

- Carbohydrates: 2g, Sodium: 223mg

13. Diabetic Stuffed Peppers Recipe

Preparation Time: 25 Minutes

Baking Time: 20 Minutes

Ingredients

- Four medium-size green peppers
- 1/2 pound extra-lean ground beef
- 1/2 cup chopped onion
- 1 cup drained, canned whole tomatoes
- 1 cup cooked wild rice

- One tablespoon Worcestershire sauce
- 1/2 teaspoon Italian seasoning
- 1/2 cup soft bread crumbs
- Vegetable cooking spray
- 1 cup canned tomato sauce

Directions

1. Slice off the stem end of peppers and remove and discard seeds and membranes.
2. Submerge the peppers in a pan of boiling water and cook for 5 to 10 minutes; drain.
3. Brown ground beef and onion in a nonstick skillet over medium heat.
4. Drain and pat dry with paper towels. Return meat mixture to skillet.
5. Add tomatoes, breaking them into pieces with a cooking spoon, and cook until liquid evaporates.
6. Remove meat mixture from heat; stir in wild rice, Worcestershire sauce, and Italian seasoning. Spoon 1/2-cup portions of rice mixture into peppers; sprinkle evenly with bread crumbs.
7. Place peppers in a baking dish coated with cooking spray. Bake at 350°F for 20 minutes or until lightly browned.
8. Spoon tomato sauce over peppers and return to oven until heated.

Nutrition Information

- Carbohydrates: 34g, Protein: 19g, Fat: 4g, Saturated Fat: <1g, Sodium: 653mg, Fiber: 5g

14. Orzo Stuffed Peppers

Preparation Time: 25 Minutes

Baking Time: 45 Minutes

Ingredients

- 8 ounces orzo or another small pasta shape
- Two teaspoons oil
- Two cloves garlic, minced
- One medium onion, chopped
- 1/2 teaspoon thyme
- One tablespoon chopped fresh parsley

- 1/2 cup grated Parmesan cheese
- 1 1/2 plus 1/2 cups low-sodium chicken broth
- 3 ounces reduced-fat provolone cheese, grated and divided into halves
- Six red bell peppers
- Three teaspoons dry bread crumbs

Directions

1. Preheat oven to 350°F.
2. Prepare pasta according to package directions; drain and set aside.
3. Heat oil in a medium saucepan; add garlic, onion, and celery.
4. Cover and cook until vegetables are soft. Remove from heat. Stir in pasta, thyme, parsley, Parmesan cheese, 1/2 cup of the chicken broth, and half of the provolone cheese.
5. Cut tops off the peppers and remove seeds. Cut a small piece off the bottoms so peppers will stand upright. Spoon the pasta mixture into each pepper and set it in a baking dish.
6. Sprinkle each pepper with 1/2 teaspoon bread crumbs. Sprinkle the remaining half of the provolone on top of the peppers.
7. Pour the remaining 1 1/2 cups of broth around peppers.
8. Bake 45 minutes until lightly browned on top and tender. Serve immediately.

Nutrition Information

- Carbohydrates: 38g, Protein: 14g, Fat: 7g, Saturated Fat: 3g, Sodium: 383mg, Fiber: 3g

15. Lemon-Pepper-Glazed Veggie Toss

Preparation Time: 20 Minutes

Cooking Time: Approximately 10 Minutes.

Ingredients

- 1/2 packet saccharin sweetener
- Two teaspoons cornstarch
- 1/4 teaspoon lemon pepper seasoning
- Two tablespoons fresh-squeezed lemon juice
- One tablespoon water
- Cooking spray
- One teaspoon corn oil
- 1 cup julienned carrots
- 3 cups cauliflower florets
- 1/4 cup water
- 1 cup asparagus sliced into 2-inch pieces

Directions

1. In a small bowl, whisk together sweetener, cornstarch, lemon pepper seasoning, lemon juice, and water. Set aside.

2. Coat an excellent, nonstick wok with cooking spray. Preheat wok, then add oil. When the oil is hot, add carrots and cook for 2 minutes, stirring constantly.

3. Add cauliflower and water and continue cooking 2 minutes more, stirring constantly.

4. Add asparagus and cook for an additional 2 minutes, stirring constantly.

5. Stir in lemon mixture and cook 20–30 seconds, or until the glaze thickens. Serve immediately.

Nutrition Information

- Carbohydrates: 4g, Protein: 2g, Fat: 1g, Saturated Fat: <1g, Sodium: 56mg, Fiber: 2g

16. Black Bean And Vegetable Enchiladas

Preparation Time: 15 Minutes

Baking Time: 20 Minutes

Ingredients

- Vegetable cooking spray
- One can plus one can (16 ounces each) black beans, rinsed and drained
- 1 cup chopped onion
- One green pepper, chopped
- Two tablespoons vegetable broth

- 1 cup plus 1 cup Picante sauce
- 12 medium corn tortillas
- 1 cup chopped tomatoes
- 1/2 cup reduced-fat shredded Cheddar cheese
- 1/2 cup reduced-fat shredded mozzarella cheese
- 3 cups shredded lettuce
- Light sour cream for garnish (optional)

Directions

1. Preheat oven to 350°F and coat a 9"x13" baking pan with vegetable cooking spray.

2. Mash one can of the beans with a spoon or in a blender or food processor; set aside.

3. Sauté the onion and green pepper in the vegetable broth until tender, about 2 to 3 minutes.

4. Add 1 cup Picante sauce, the mashed beans, and the can of whole beans.

5. Stir the mixture and heat thoroughly. Spoon about 1/3 cup of the bean mixture down the center of each tortilla and roll it up.

6. Place the tortillas seam-side down in the baking pan. Combine the remaining cup of Picante sauce and the tomatoes; spoon over enchiladas. Cover with foil and bake for 15 minutes. Uncover, sprinkle with cheeses, and bake, uncovered, for five more minutes. To serve, place 1/2 cup

lettuce on each plate and top with two enchiladas. Garnish with sour cream, if desired.

Nutrition Information

- Carbohydrates: 59g, Protein: 15g, Fat: 5g, Saturated Fat: 2g, Sodium: 807mg, Fiber: 12g

17. Zesty Broccoli Salad

Preparation Time: 15 Minutes

Chilling Time: 1–2 Hours

Ingredients

- 4 cups fresh small broccoli florets
- 1 cup thinly sliced purple onion rings
- 1/2 cup sweetened, dried cranberries
- 1/2 cup reduced-fat Italian dressing

- Two tablespoons dry-roasted sunflower seeds

Directions

1. Combine all ingredients in a serving dish and toss to coat well. Refrigerate for 1–2 hours to allow flavors to blend.
2. Toss again before serving.

Nutrition Information

- Carbohydrates: 10g, Protein: 2g, Fat: 3g, Saturated Fat: <1g, Sodium: 110mg, Fiber:2g

18. Exotic Amaretto Maroon Carrots

Preparation Time: 10 Minutes

Cooking Time: 8–9 Minutes.

Ingredients

- 1 pound maroon carrots (who can substitute plain carrots)
- Two tablespoons water
- 1 1/2 tablespoons reduced-calorie stick margarine, melted
- One tablespoon Amaretto

Directions

1. Peel carrots and slice them into 1-inch pieces.
2. Place in a microwave-safe dish, add two tablespoons of water and cover with a lid or microwave-safe plastic wrap.
3. Microwave on 100% for 8–9 minutes, or until tender when pierced with a fork. Drain water.
4. In a small bowl, stir together melted margarine and Amaretto.
5. Drizzle evenly over carrots and toss to coat.

Nutrition Information

- Carbohydrates: 12g, Protein: 1g, Fat: 3g, Saturated Fat: 1g, Sodium: 50mg, Fiber: 4g

19. Country-Style Collard Greens

Preparation Time: 15 Minutes

Cooking Time: 50–55 Minutes.

Ingredients

- One tablespoon corn oil
- 1/2 cup chopped onion (about one small onion)
- One teaspoon (or one clove) minced garlic
- 1 pound collard greens, trimmed and chopped (about two large bunches)
- Two cans (14.5 ounces each) fat-free, reduced-sodium chicken broth

- One teaspoon packed brown sugar
- 1 1/2 teaspoons liquid smoke flavoring
- 1/4 teaspoon red pepper flakes

Directions

1. Heat oil in a large pot.
2. Add onion and garlic and cook, frequently stirring, until onion is tender, taking care not to burn the garlic.
3. Add greens, chicken broth, brown sugar, liquid smoke flavoring, and red pepper flakes.
4. Cover, bring to a boil, reduce heat to medium and simmer 30 minutes, or until greens are tender; stir periodically.
5. Remove the lid from the pan and continue cooking until most of the liquid evaporates (about 15–20 minutes more).

Nutrition Information

- Carbohydrates: 10g, Protein: 3g, Fat: 4g, Saturated Fat: 1g, Sodium: 550mg, Fiber: 3g

20. Luscious Lentils

Preparation Time: 15 Minutes

Soaking Time: 1 Hour

Cooking Time: Approximately 1 3/4 Hours

Ingredients

- 2 cups dried lentils, rinsed and picked over for small stones or debris
- 3 quarts cold water
- 6 cups low-sodium chicken broth
- 2 1/2 cups water
- One can (14 1/2 ounces) no-salt-added diced tomatoes, undrained
- Two teaspoons olive oil
- One large onion, finely chopped
- 1/2 teaspoon dried thyme
- One teaspoon minced garlic
- 1/4 teaspoon coarse ground black pepper
- One tablespoon dried parsley
- 1/2 cup plus one tablespoon chopped green onions (approximately five green onions)
- Six tablespoons reduced-fat sour cream

Directions

1. Soak lentils in the 3 quarts of cold water for 1 hour.
2. Drain. In a large pan, combine soaked lentils, broth, 2 1/2 cups water, tomatoes, olive oil, onion, thyme, and garlic; stir to mix.
3. Cover and bring to a boil over high heat. Reduce heat to medium and simmer for about 1 1/2 hours, or until lentils are tender.
4. Stir periodically, add more water if a thinner broth is desired, or cook on medium-low for thicker consistency (some broth should remain).
5. Stir in pepper and parsley, and simmer 5 minutes longer.
6. Serve alone or over-cooked brown rice.
7. Top each serving with one tablespoon green onions and two teaspoons sour cream.

Nutrition Information

- Carbohydrates: 35g, Protein: 17g, Fat: 3g, Saturated Fat: 1g, Sodium: 72mg, Fiber: 7g

21. Dill Green Beans

Preparation Time: 5 Minutes

Cooking Time: Approximately 10 Minutes.

Ingredients

- 6 cups water

- One package (14 ounces) frozen whole green beans, thawed
- Two tablespoons extra virgin olive oil
- Two tablespoons cider vinegar
- 1/4 cup finely chopped green onion
- Two tablespoons chopped fresh dill
- 1/4 teaspoon salt
- 1/4 teaspoon black pepper

Directions

1. Bring water to boil in a large saucepan; add green beans and cook about 10 minutes or until tender when pierced with a fork (beans should retain their bright green color).
2. Meanwhile, in a small bowl, whisk together olive oil, vinegar, green onion, dill, salt, and pepper. Drain cooked beans well.
3. Drizzle dill sauce over the beans and toss gently to coat well.

Nutrition Information

- Carbohydrates: 3g, Protein: 1g, Fat: 3g, Saturated Fat: <1g, Sodium: 60mg, Fiber: 1g

22. Beef Bean Burgers

Preparation Time: 15 Minutes

Cooking Time: 4–6 Minutes.

Standing Time: 15 Minutes

Ingredients

- One can (15 ounces) pinto beans, rinsed and drained
- 1/2 15-ounce can black beans, rinsed and drained
- 1/2 cup uncooked quick-cooking oats
- 1/4 cup liquid egg substitute
- 1/4 cup no-salt-added ketchup
- 1/8 teaspoon garlic powder

- 1/4 teaspoon liquid smoke
- Two dashes of cayenne pepper
- Two green onions, finely chopped
- Cooking spray
- Two tablespoons corn oil

Directions

1. Combine rinsed and drained pinto and black beans in a large bowl; mash well using a potato masher.
2. Stir in oats, egg substitute, ketchup, garlic powder, liquid smoke, cayenne pepper, and green onions; mix well. Allow mixture to stand 15 minutes to thicken, then shape into 5 (4-inch) patties approximately 1/2-inch in thickness.
3. Coat a large, nonstick skillet with cooking spray, add oil, and warm over medium to medium-high heat.
4. Add burgers and cook 2–3 minutes on each side, or until lightly browned; turn using a large spatula to prevent burgers from breaking apart.
5. Serve on whole-wheat buns topped with favorite burger toppings.

Nutrition Information

- Carbohydrates: 29g, Protein: 9g, Fat: 7g, Saturated Fat: 1g, Sodium: 305mg, Fiber: 8g

23. Instant Refried Beans Recipe For Diabetics

Preparation Time: 20 minutes

Ingredients

- 1 pound dried pinto beans
- 1/2 tablespoon chili powder
- One tablespoon ground cumin
- 1/8 teaspoon garlic powder
- Two dashes of cayenne pepper
- Two teaspoons salt
- One tablespoon dried minced onion
- 2 1/2 cups water

Directions

1. Preheat oven to 350°F. Look beans over and discard any foreign material.
2. Quickly rinse beans and drain well to prevent them from absorbing water. Turn beans out on a dry towel and pat dry.
3. Place beans in a single layer in a 9" x 13" baking pan and bake 4–5 minutes, frequently stirring, to dry beans. Pour beans out onto a dry towel to cool to room temperature.

4. Using a blender, coffee grinder (make sure it's free of coffee bean powder), or food mill, process cooled beans in small batches until they're the consistency of flour (larger lumps will add crunch to your beans).
5. Pour processed beans into a bowl and add remaining dry ingredients.
6. Stir until well mixed. Store in an airtight container until ready to prepare.
7. You will have about 3 cups of bean mix.

To Prepare:

1. Place 2 1/2 cups water in a medium-size saucepan and bring to a boil over high heat.
2. Add 3/4 cup bean mix to boiling water and mix with a wire whisk until combined. There may be a few lumps that add texture.
3. Return to a boil over medium-high heat, cover, reduce heat to low-medium and simmer for 11–12 minutes, or until thickened; periodically remove the lid and stir beans.
4. Beans will continue to thicken as they cool. Thin, as needed, with hot water.

Nutrition Information

- Carbohydrates: 15g, Protein: 5g, Fat: <1g, Sodium: 245mg, Fiber: 9g

24. Spicy Black Bean Burritos

Preparation Time: 25 Minutes

Ingredients

- Two cans (15 ounces each) black beans, rinsed and drained
- 1 cup frozen corn, thawed
- 1 cup cooked rice
- 16 ounces mild Picante sauce
- 1/4 teaspoon lime juice
- 1/4 teaspoon ground cumin
- 10 (8-inch) flour tortillas
- Fat-free sour cream (optional)

Directions

1. Place beans in a nonstick skillet over medium heat. Mash about half of the beans with a fork or the back of a spoon.
2. Add corn, rice, Picante sauce, lime juice, and cumin. Stir to combine. Cook over medium heat, frequently stirring, until hot and bubbly.
3. Warm tortillas, if desired. Spoon 1/2 cup bean mixture down the center of each flour tortilla. Fold tortilla around filling.
4. Top with a dollop of fat-free sour cream if desired.
5. Bean filling can be made ahead and frozen or refrigerated until serving time.
6. Warm over low-medium heat on the stove or in the microwave.

Nutrition Information

- Carbohydrates: 66g, Protein: 10g, Fat: 4g, Saturated Fat: <1g, Sodium: 995mg, Fiber: 5g

25. Diabetic Summer Squash Side Dish Recipe

Preparation Time: 10 Minutes

Cooking Time: Approximately 7 Minutes.

Ingredients

- Cooking spray
- One teaspoon olive oil
- Four small yellow squash (approximately 5 inches long), quartered and sliced 1/4-inch thick (about 2 cups total)

- Two medium zucchini (around 6-7 inches long), quartered and sliced 1/4-inch wide (about 2 cups total)
- 1 cup thinly sliced onion, separated into rings
- 3/4 teaspoon parslied garlic salt

Directions

1. Coat an excellent, nonstick wok with cooking spray. Preheat wok, then add oil.
2. When the oil is hot, add yellow squash, zucchini, and onion.
3. Cook, constantly stirring, for 4-5 minutes, or until the squash is crisp-tender.
4. Sprinkle with parslied garlic salt and toss to coat.
5. Serve immediately.

Nutrition Information

- Carbohydrates: 5g, Protein: 1g, Fat: 1g, Saturated Fat: <1g, Sodium: 222 mg, Fiber: 1g

26. Asparagus With Mustard Vinaigrette

Preparation Time: 20 Minutes

Ingredients

- 1 pound fresh asparagus, preferably thin spears
- Two teaspoons Dijon-style mustard
- Three tablespoons red wine vinegar
- One teaspoon granulated sugar
- 1/4 teaspoon salt
- 1/4 teaspoon black pepper
- One tablespoon minced fresh parsley
- Two tablespoons olive oil

Directions

1. Wash asparagus and trim the ends.
2. If stems are tough, remove the outer layer with a vegetable peeler.
3. Drop asparagus into boiling water and cook approximately 8 minutes or until desired texture is reached; drain.
4. Measure mustard into a bowl.
5. Whisk in vinegar, sugar, salt, pepper, and parsley. Whisk in olive oil until the mixture is blended. Pour over cooked asparagus.

6. Serve warm.

Nutrition Information

- Carbohydrates: 3g, Protein: 1g, Fat: 5g, Saturated Fat: <1g, Sodium: 121mg, Fiber: 1g

27. Black Beans And Rice

Preparation Time: 20 Minutes

Ingredients

- One can (15 ounces) black beans, undrained
- 1/4 teaspoon garlic salt
- Two dashes of cayenne pepper
- 1/4 teaspoon lime juice
- One can (14.5 ounces) diced tomatoes seasoned with basil, garlic, and oregano
- 3 cups cooked brown rice

- 1/2 ripe avocado (about 5 ounces), chopped into bite-size pieces
- 1/4 cup crumbled garlic-herb or plain Feta cheese

Directions

1. Place beans with their liquid in a small saucepan and stir in garlic salt, cayenne pepper, and lime juice.
2. Simmer over medium heat until heated through.
3. In another small saucepan, warm tomatoes over medium heat until heated through.
4. Put 3/4 cup hot rice on each plate and top with one-fourth of the beans and one-fourth of the tomatoes.
5. Sprinkle each serving with one-fourth of the chopped avocado and one-fourth of the cheese.

Nutrition Information

- Carbohydrates: 60g, Protein: 12g, Fat: 9g, Saturated Fat: 3g, Sodium: 1,190mg, Fiber: 10g

28. Ginger-Caraway Carrots

Preparation Time: 15–20 Minutes

Ingredients

- Two tablespoons butter or margarine, melted
- Two tablespoons brown sugar
- 1/2 teaspoon ground ginger
- 1/2 teaspoon caraway seeds
- 1 pound peeled baby carrots

Directions

1. Mix butter or margarine, brown sugar, ginger, and caraway seeds. Set aside.
2. Place carrots in a microwave-safe dish. Add about 2 to 3 tablespoons of water to cover the bottom of the word.
3. Cover the dish with a lid or plastic wrap.
4. Microwave on High until tender, approximately 8 to 10 minutes, stirring halfway through cooking time.
5. Remove the container from the microwave and drain any water that remains.
6. Add sauce, toss to cover carrots, and return to microwave; cook on High for 1 minute.
7. Remove from microwave, stir, and place carrots in a serving dish.

Nutrition Information

- Carbohydrates: 13g, Protein: <1g, Fat: 4g, Saturated Fat: <1g, Sodium: 74mg, Fiber: 2g

29. Stir-Fried Snow Peas

Preparation Time: 15 Minutes

Cooking Time: Approximately 7 Minutes.

Ingredients

- Cooking spray
- One teaspoon sesame oil (who may substitute corn oil or canola oil)
- 3/4 pound snow peas, strings removed
- 1/4 teaspoon salt

Directions

1. Coat an excellent, nonstick wok with cooking spray.

2. Preheat wok, then add oil. When the oil is hot, add snow peas.
3. Cook, constantly stirring, for 4–5 minutes, or until pods are crisp-tender.
4. Sprinkle with salt and toss to coat. Serve immediately.

Nutrition Information

- Carbohydrates: 4g, Protein: 1g, Fat: 1g, Saturated Fat: <1g, Sodium: 97mg, Fiber: 1g

30. Lemon-Pepper-Glazed Veggie Toss

Preparation Time: 20 Minutes

Cooking Time: Approximately 10 Minutes.

Ingredients

- 1/2 packet saccharin sweetener
- Two teaspoons cornstarch
- 1/4 teaspoon lemon pepper seasoning
- Two tablespoons fresh-squeezed lemon juice
- One tablespoon water
- Cooking spray
- One teaspoon corn oil
- 1 cup julienned carrots
- 3 cups cauliflower florets
- 1/4 cup water
- 1 cup asparagus sliced into 2-inch pieces

Directions

1. In a small bowl, whisk together sweetener, cornstarch, lemon pepper seasoning, lemon juice, and water. Set aside.
2. Coat an excellent, nonstick wok with cooking spray.

3. Preheat wok, then add oil. When the oil is hot, add carrots and cook for 2 minutes, stirring constantly.

4. Add cauliflower and water and continue cooking 2 minutes more, stirring constantly.

5. Add asparagus and cook for an additional 2 minutes, stirring constantly.

6. Stir in lemon mixture and cook 20–30 seconds, or until the glaze thickens.

7. Serve immediately.

Nutrition Information

- Carbohydrates: 4g, Protein: 2g, Fat: 1g, Saturated Fat: <1g, Sodium: 56mg, Fiber: 2g

31. Corny Zucchini Medley

Preparation Time: 10 Minutes

Cooking Time: Approximately 15 Minutes.

Standing Time: 4–5 Minutes

Ingredients

- Cooking spray
- 1 1/2 teaspoons olive oil
- One clove garlic, minced
- One small onion, finely chopped

- Two dashes of hot pepper sauce (such as Tabasco)
- 2 cups frozen corn, thawed
- 2 cups chopped zucchini (approximately 9 ounces)
- 1/3 cup finely shredded, reduced-fat Monterey Jack cheese
- Four slices of turkey bacon, cooked, drained, and crumbled
- 1/4 cup finely diced tomato

Directions

1. Coat a nonstick skillet with cooking spray, add olive oil, and warm over medium heat.
2. Add garlic and onion; cook, frequently stirring, for 2–3 minutes, or until onion is translucent.
3. Stir in hot pepper sauce.
4. Add corn and zucchini and cook until crisp-tender, about 10 minutes; stir frequently.
5. Spoon vegetables into a serving dish and sprinkle evenly with cheese, bacon, and tomato.
6. Allow standing 4–5 minutes for the cheese to melt.

Nutrition Information

- Carbohydrates: 13g, Protein: 5g, Fat: 4g, Saturated Fat: 1g, Sodium: 147mg, Fiber: 2g

32. Artichoke Sandwich Spread

Preparation Time: 5 Minutes

Chilling Time: 1 Hour

Ingredients

- 8 ounces fat-free cream cheese
- Two tablespoons light mayonnaise (not salad dressing–style mayonnaise)
- 1 cup drained marinated artichoke hearts, finely chopped
- Two tablespoons marinade from artichokes

Directions

1. Place cream cheese in a mixing bowl and whip with an electric mixer until fluffy.
2. Whip in mayonnaise. Stir in chopped artichoke hearts and marinade.
3. Store in an airtight container in the refrigerator and chill for at least 1 hour to allow flavors to blend.
4. Spread on thinly sliced whole wheat bread.

Nutrition Information

- Carbohydrates: 2g, Protein: 3g, Fat: 2g, Saturated Fat: <1g, Sodium: 117mg

33. Seasoned Brussels Sprouts

Preparation Time: 25 Minutes

Ingredients

- 6 cups water
- 1 pound tiny Brussels sprouts
- Three tablespoons reduced-calorie margarine
- One green onion, finely chopped
- One teaspoon (or one clove) minced garlic
- One teaspoon salt
- 1/8 teaspoon ground ginger

- One tablespoon slivered almonds, toasted and chopped

Directions

1. Bring the 6 cups of water to a boil in a large pan. Add the Brussels sprouts to the boiling water.
2. Cook 6–7 minutes (or until tender when pierced with a fork; do not overcook), then drain well.
3. Meanwhile, cut an "x" in the stem end of the sprouts for more even cooking. Set aside.
4. Melt margarine in a large, nonstick skillet over medium heat.
5. Add green onion, garlic, salt, and ginger.
6. Cook, frequently stirring until onion softens.
7. Add sprouts and gently toss to coat. Heat 1–2 minutes, then sprinkle with toasted almonds.

Nutrition Information

- Carbohydrates: 8g, Protein: 3g, Fat: 4g, Saturated Fat: 1g, Sodium: 460mg, Fiber: 3g

34. Green Bean And Red Pepper Sauté

Preparation Time: 30 Minutes

Ingredients

- 1 pound fresh green beans, ends trimmed
- Two tablespoons olive oil
- One large red bell pepper, cut into strips
- One teaspoon lemon juice
- 1/4 cup chopped salted cashews
- Dash of black pepper

Directions

1. In a large kettle, bring 3 quarts of water to a boil.

2. Add green beans and return water to a spot.

3. Cook, uncovered, for 8 to 10 minutes until crisp-tender.

4. Plunge beans into cold water to stop cooking.

5. Beans may be covered and refrigerated overnight at this point. Heat oil in a large saucepan or wok until hot.

6. Sauté red pepper over medium heat for 2 to 3 minutes. Stir in beans, lemon juice, cashews, and pepper.

7. Cook and stir gently until thoroughly heated, about 6 to 8 minutes.

8. Transfer to a serving platter and serve immediately.

Nutrition Information

- Carbohydrates: 7g, Protein: 2g, Fat: 7g, Saturated Fat: 1g, Sodium: 40mg, Fiber: 2g

35. Balsamic-Basil Sliced Tomatoes

Preparation Time: 10 Minutes

Ingredients

- Two medium ripe tomatoes (about 4 ounces each) or one large tomato (about 8 ounces)

- One teaspoon olive oil
- One tablespoon balsamic vinegar
- 1/8 teaspoon coarse ground black pepper
- 1/4 cup snipped fresh basil
- Two tablespoons finely crumbled garlic-herb Feta cheese (who can substitute plain Feta)

Directions

1. Slice tomatoes and lay them on a serving platter.
2. Drizzle evenly with olive oil and balsamic vinegar. Sprinkle evenly with cracked pepper, snipped basil, and cheese.
3. Divide into four equal portions and serve right away.

Nutrition Information

- Carbohydrates: 4g, Protein: 1g, Fat: 2g, Saturated Fat: 1g, Sodium: 60mg, Fiber: 1g

36. Tangy Steamed Green Bean Salad

Preparation Time: 10 Minutes

Cooking Time: 7 Minutes

Ingredients

- 1 pound fresh whole green beans, washed, ends trimmed off
- Two tablespoons extra-virgin olive oil
- Two tablespoons red wine vinegar
- One tablespoon Dijon-style mustard
- One tablespoon water
- 1/4 teaspoon garlic powder
- 1/4 teaspoon black pepper
- Four green onions, finely chopped
- Ten cherry tomatoes, cut in half

Directions

1. Steam green beans in a steamer (or use a steaming basket in a saucepan) for about 5 minutes until bright green and still slightly crisp.

2. Immediately rinse under cold running water until cool to the touch.
3. Drain. Place in a serving dish. In a small bowl, combine olive oil, red wine vinegar, mustard, water, and garlic powder with a small whisk or spoon.
4. Pour over green beans.
5. Add green onions and tomatoes, toss well, and serve.

Nutrition Information

- Carbohydrates: 12g, Protein: 3g, Fat: 7g, Sodium: 62mg, Fiber: 5g

37. Squash And Corn

Preparation Time: 10 Minutes

Cooking Time: 20–25 Minutes.

Ingredients

- 1 pound zucchini, sliced lengthwise
- Three roasted green chilies, peeled and seeded (who used banana peppers in testing; alternatively, half a four 1/2-ounce can of roasted, diced chilies can be used)
- Cooking spray
- One teaspoon corn oil
- One small onion, finely chopped
- One teaspoon of real bacon bits

- 2 cups frozen corn, thawed (who can also use fresh corn cut from the cob)
- 1/4 cup water
- 1/4 teaspoon salt

Directions

1. Dice zucchini into 1/2-inch pieces.
2. Thinly slice chilies. Coat a large nonstick skillet with cooking spray, add oil, and warm over medium-high heat.
3. Add onion and cook, frequently stirring, until translucent, about 3–4 minutes.
4. Add bacon bits and corn and cook 2–3 minutes more, stirring frequently. Add water, squash, chilies, and salt; stir to mix.
5. Cover pan, reduce heat to medium, and simmer 10–15 minutes, or until corn and zucchini are tender; stir occasionally.

Nutrition Information

- Carbohydrates: 11g, Protein: 3g, Fat: 1g, Saturated Fat: <1g, Cholesterol: <1mg, Sodium: 91mg, Fiber: 2g

38. Black Bean And Rice Recipe For Diabetics

Preparation Time: 20 Minutes

Ingredients

- 1 (15-ounce) can black beans, rinsed and drained
- 1 (12-ounce) jar thick and chunky mild salsa
- 1 (8 3/4-ounce) can no-salt-added corn, drained
- 4 cups cooked brown rice
- 1 cup (4 ounces) shredded Monterey Jack cheese

Directions

1. Combine black beans, salsa, and corn in a saucepan and warm over medium heat until bubbly (approximately 10 minutes).
2. Spoon 1/2 cup bean mixture over 1/2 cup hot, cooked rice. Sprinkle with two tablespoons of cheese and serve.

Nutrition Information

- Carbohydrates: 59g, Protein: 11g, Fat: 6g, Saturated Fat: 2g, Sodium: 444mg, Fiber: 4g

39. Gingered Snow Peas

Preparation Time: 2 Minutes

Ingredients

- 6 ounces fresh snow peas
- Two medium carrots (6–8 inches in length)
- One teaspoon peanut oil
- One tablespoon minced shallots
- One teaspoon minced ginger
- One teaspoon lite (low-sodium) soy sauce

Directions

1. Wash and drain snow peas.
2. Remove pod string with a sharp knife if necessary.
3. Using a vegetable peeler, shave the carrots into thin strips until you reach the inner core layer of the carrot; discard the core.
4. You should get about 1/2 cup or more of shavings from the two carrots.
5. Heat peanut oil in a medium skillet or wok over medium-high heat.
6. Add shallots and ginger and stir, then add snow peas and stir-fry for approximately 2 minutes until peas are bright green and still crisp.

7. Next, add soy sauce and carrot shavings and stir-fry for only 30–60 seconds more. (Overcooking the carrots will cause them to shrink considerably.)

Nutrition Information

- Carbohydrates: 7g, Protein: 2g, Fat: 1g, Sodium: 69 mg, Fiber: 2g

40. Roasted Winter Vegetable Blend

Preparation Time: 15 Minutes

Ingredients

- Two medium carrots, peeled
- One medium sweet potato, peeled

- One large russet potato
- One medium turnip, peeled
- One medium parsnip, peeled
- One large onion, peeled
- Two tablespoons tomato paste
- One tablespoon olive oil
- Two teaspoons Italian herb blend
- Black pepper to taste

Directions

1. Preheat oven to 400°F. Cut carrots, sweet potato, potato, turnip, parsnip, and onion into chunks.
2. Place in a large bowl.
3. Mix tomato paste and olive oil into vegetables, stirring well to coat all surfaces.
4. Sprinkle with an herb blend and black pepper.
5. Spread on the shallow baking sheet or pan so that vegetables are in a single layer.
6. Bake 40–45 minutes, turning vegetables once with a spatula during cooking, until vegetables are fork-tender.

Nutrition Information

Carbohydrates: 26g, Protein: 2g, Fat: 2g, Sodium: 45mg, Fiber: 4g